Gross Things: From Your Head to Your Toes

Pauline Cartwright

Contents

We're Gross 2
Creepy Crawlies 4
Love Your Earwax 6
Up Your Nose 10
Gross Things in Your Mouth 14
Your Gut 16
It Stinks! 22
Sweaty, Smelly Feet 24
Your Gross Trail 26
Gross Stuff 28
All Things Gross 30
Glossary 31
Index 32

We're Gross

My mum thinks I'm clean but I'm really **gross**.
We are all **gross** from our heads to our toes.
Get ready to read about **gross** things inside and outside our bodies.

Before we start, you need to know this. Millions of creepy crawlies live on and in each of us! These creepy crawlies use us as a kind of **skyscraper** home. They're busy eating and pooing and we don't even know it.

Creepy Crawlies

Many of these creepy crawlies are **bacteria**. Bacteria are too small to see without a **microscope**. That's why we don't see them crawling over our skin.

Gross Fact 1

Over 500 different kinds of bacteria live on and in our bodies.

Bacteria come in different shapes and sizes. Some are round. Some are long. Some look a bit like worms!

Love your Earwax

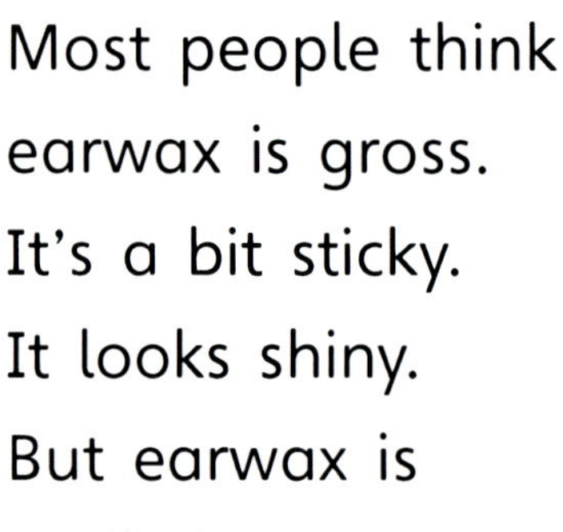

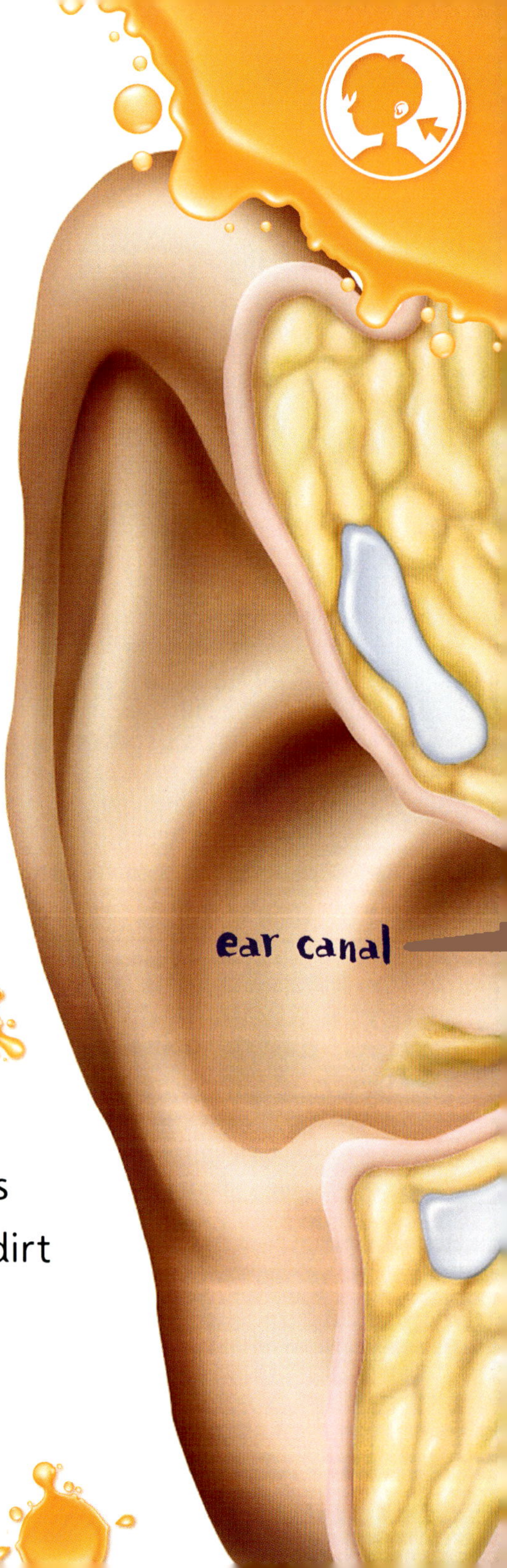

Most people think earwax is gross. It's a bit sticky. It looks shiny. But earwax is really important.

ear canal

Earwax protects your **ear canal** by acting as a trap. Earwax stops dirt and other things from going inside your ear.

So DON'T clean your ears. Never put anything in your ear to get earwax out. Your ears need that gunk!

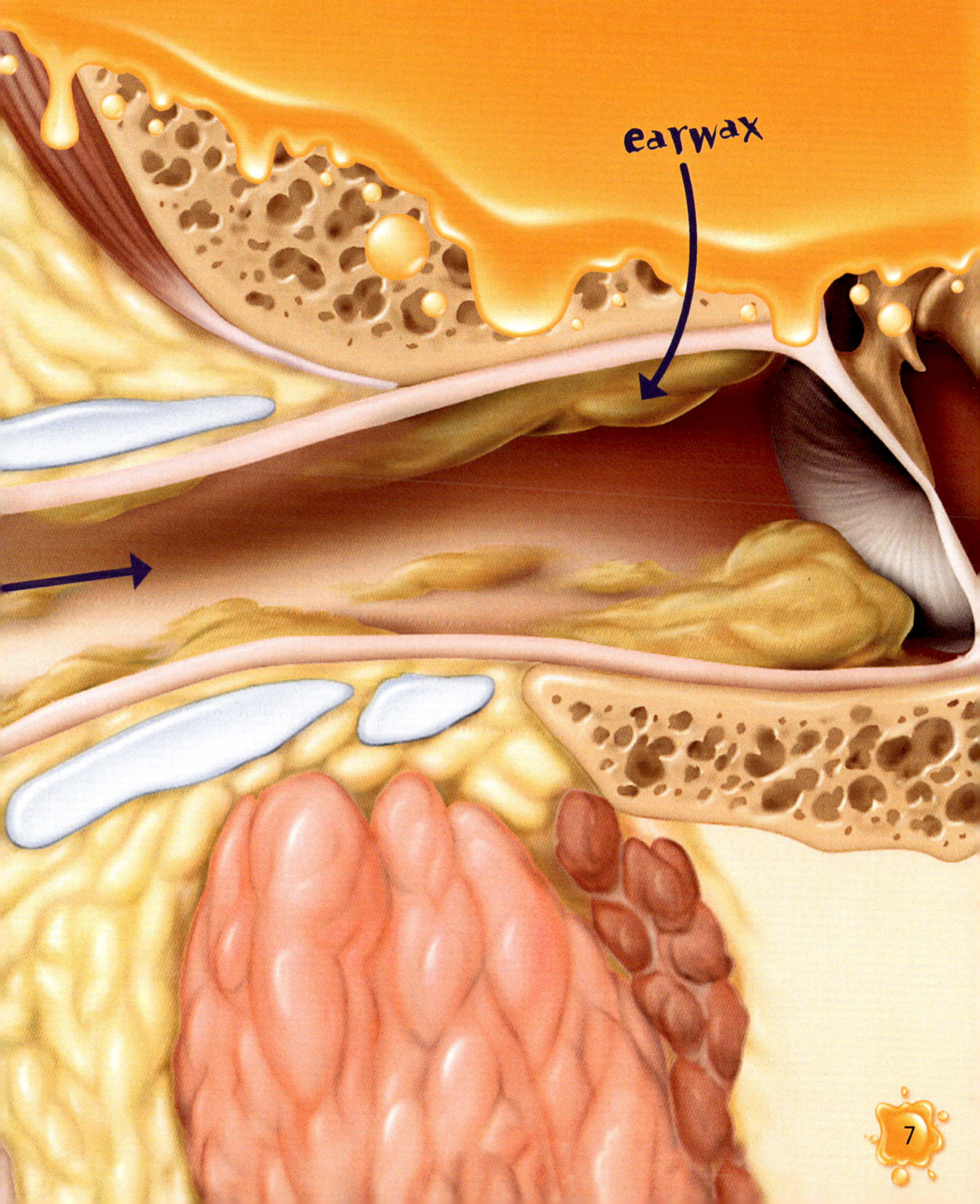

Your ears make new wax all the time. The new wax pushes out the old wax. Earwax falls out in tiny flakes. It falls out when you wash your hair. It falls out when you play sport. It falls out when you do your homework. **Gross!**

This is what earwax looks like under a microscope!
Gross Fact 2
Earwax can be many different colours. It can be grey, brown, green or even orange.

Up Your Nose

So now let's look up your nose. Your nose has lots of **gross** stuff in it. It's called **mucus**. You might call it snot. **Gross!**

Mucus is made by special **membranes**. It's not just your nose that has these membranes. Your lips, ears and mouth also have them, too.

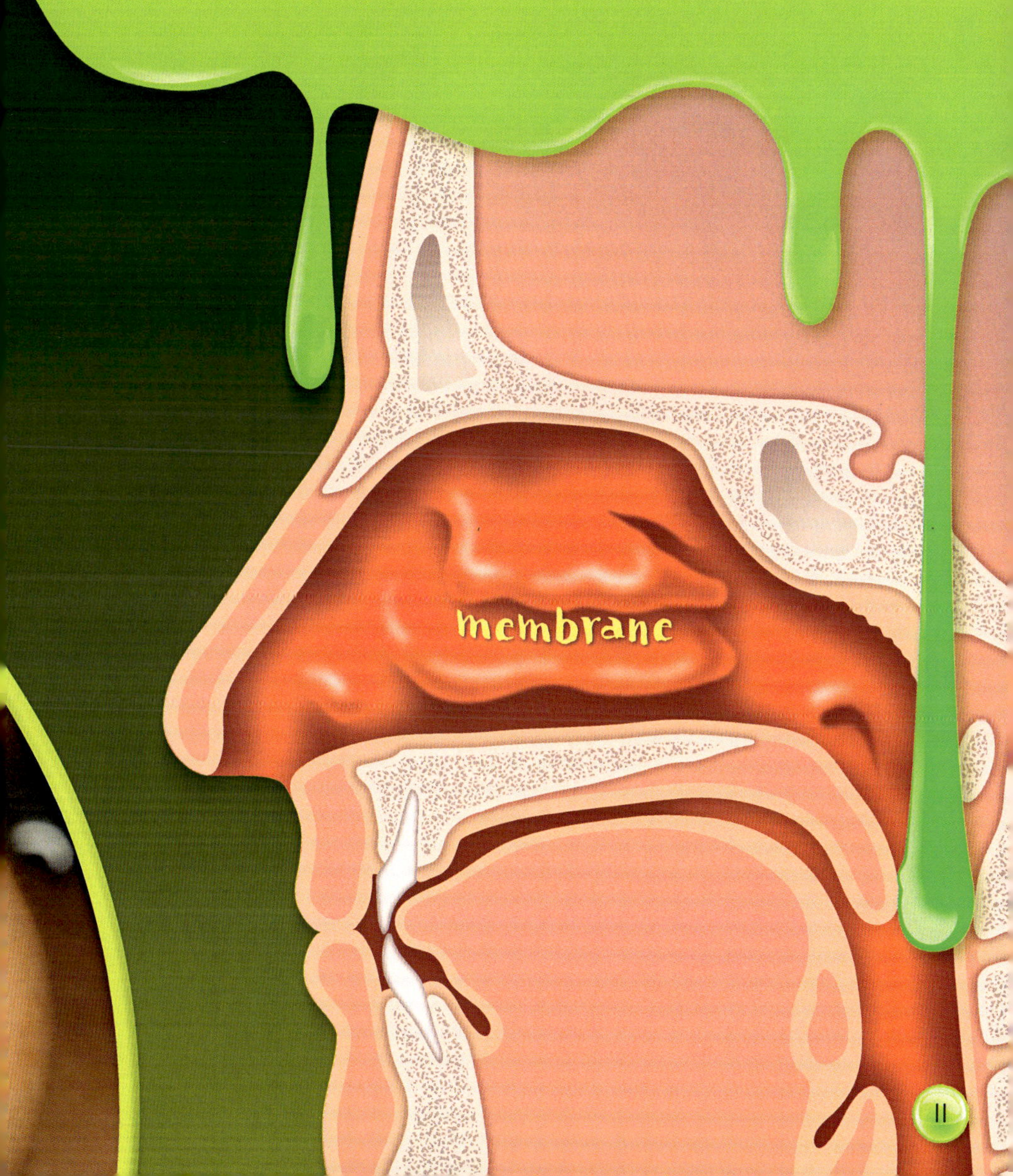

Mucus is important. It helps to clean and protect your nose. Mucus also acts as a trap. It stops dust and dirt in the air from going too far up your nose.

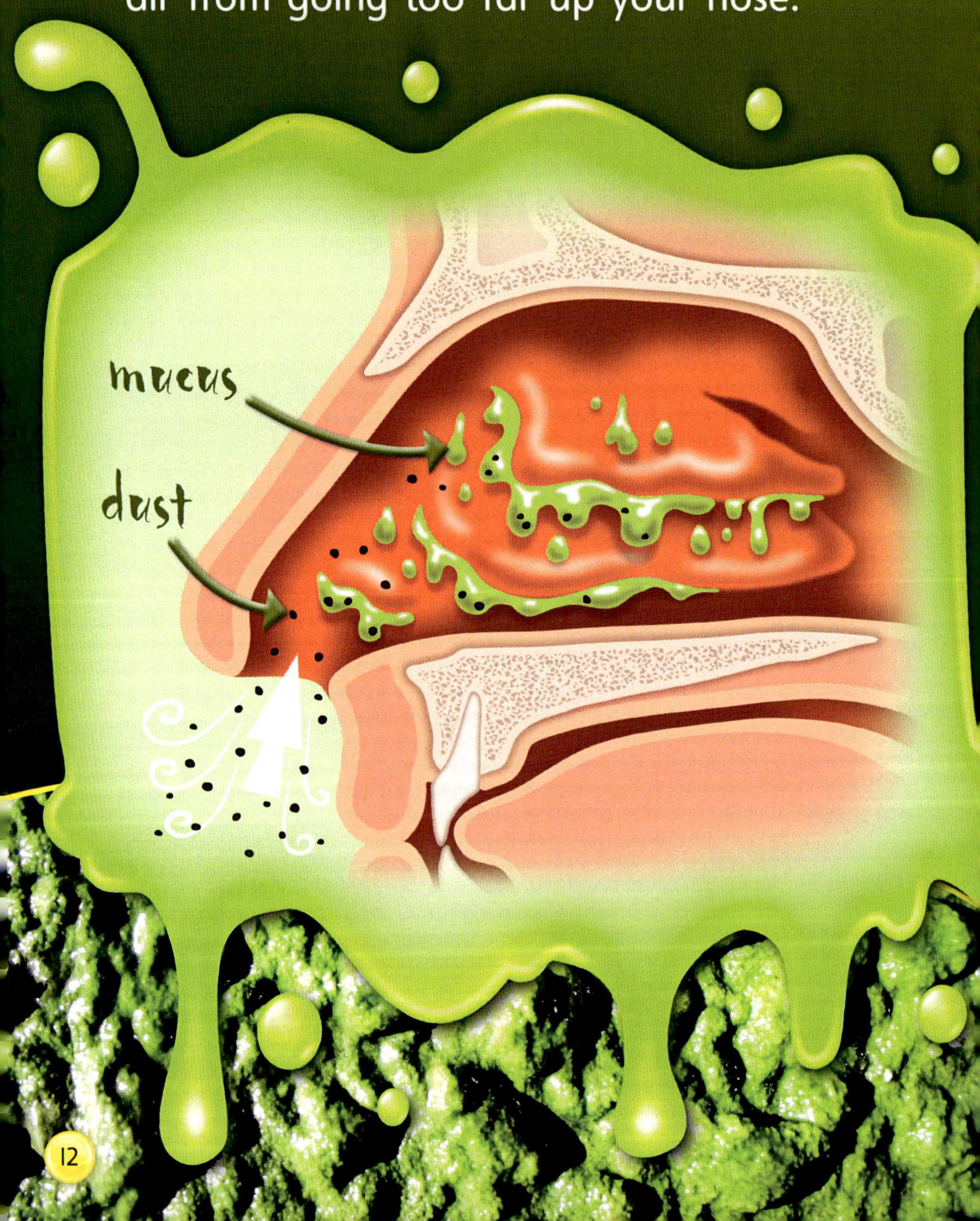

Snot

When you have a cold, you can get a runny nose. The runny mucus helps to wash bacteria out of your nose. Even when we don't have a cold, our noses make a lot of mucus. Every day, our noses make about four cups of mucus!

Gross Things in Your Mouth

Bacteria live in your mouth. They love sugar. When you eat something, some sugar stays in your mouth.

Bacteria eat the sugar. **Good!** But then the bacteria leave a chemical in your mouth. **Bad!** This **acid** can cause your teeth to decay. We have to clean our teeth to get rid of the acid. Every day.

Your stomach has a **lining** of mucus. But this mucus is different to your nose mucus. This mucus stops stomach acid from getting into your body.

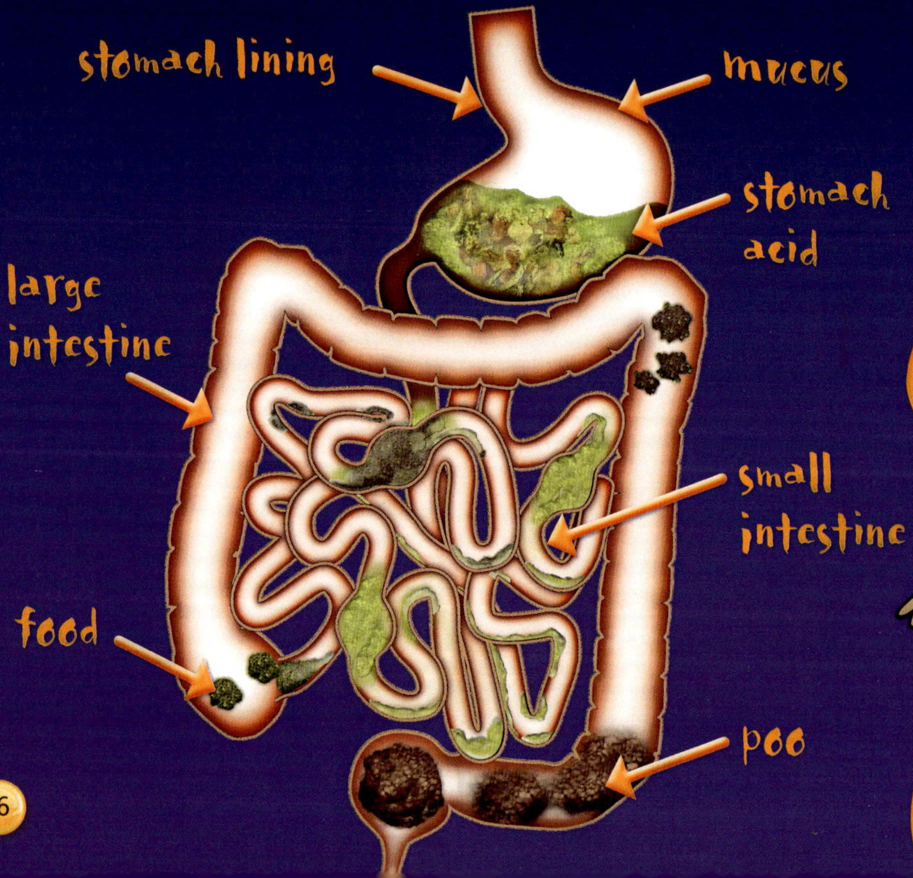

stomach lining

mucus

stomach acid

large intestine

small intestine

food

poo

Stomach acid helps to break down the food you've eaten. Stomach acid is so powerful that it can eat through metal. Thank goodness for the lining of mucus. Holes in your stomach would not be fun!

Do you sometimes hear your stomach gurgle? This is your stomach sloshing food, gas and stomach liquids around. Your stomach might be telling you something.

Gross Fact 3

A fart is the release of gas in our stomachs. Most people fart about 14 times a day!

Did you eat **too much** party food?

Did you eat something **bad?**

Turn over to find out what happens...

Throwing Up

You feel sick and your stomach begins to cramp. The cramps squeeze down on your stomach and then, **wham!** The food comes back from your stomach, into your mouth.

Out flies the vomit! Vomit is made up of mushy food, stomach liquids and spit. **Gross!**

vomit

It Stinks!

Bacteria do some useful things in your **intestines**. The bacteria help to keep your intestines clean. That keeps your insides healthy.

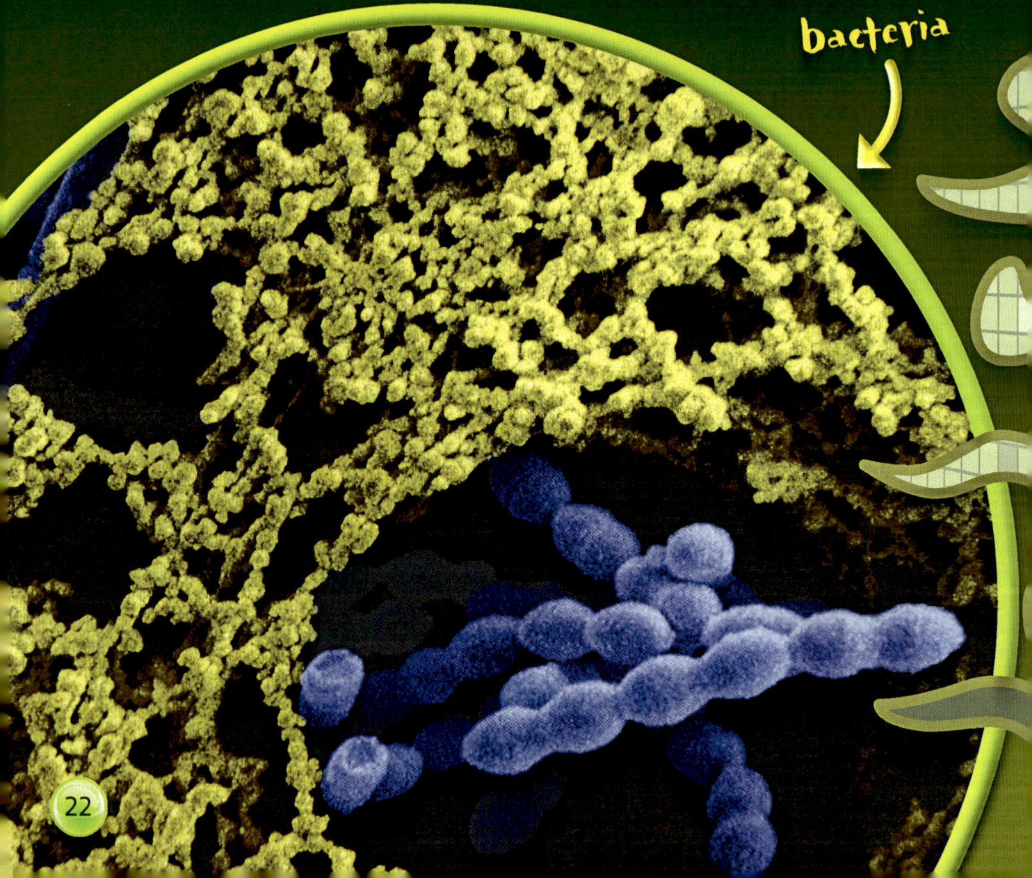

bacteria

Bacteria work hard by breaking down the food inside us. But that makes chemicals which stink. This is what makes poo smell so **gross!**

Sweaty, Smelly Feet

Bacteria also like to feed on your sweaty feet. On each foot you have thousands of **sweat glands**. They can make nearly two cups of sweat every day. **Gross!**

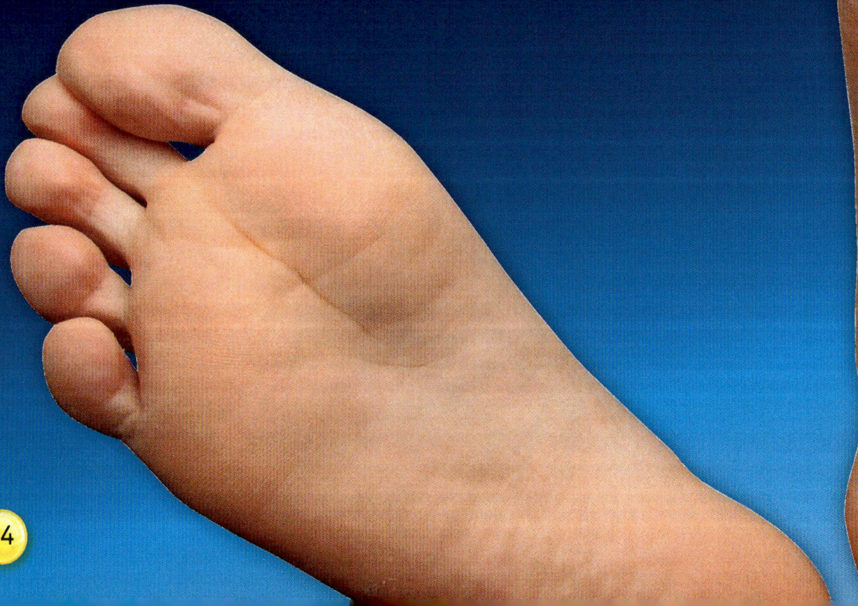

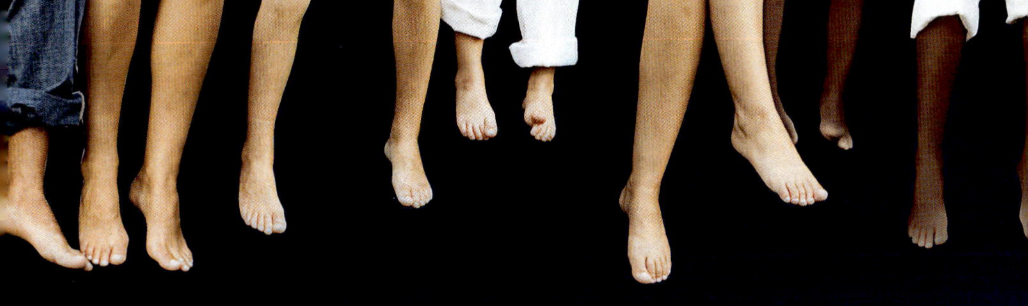

Bacteria that live on your feet love sweat. But when bacteria mix with the sweat it can make a bad smell. That's why your feet smell sometimes. Blame the bacteria!

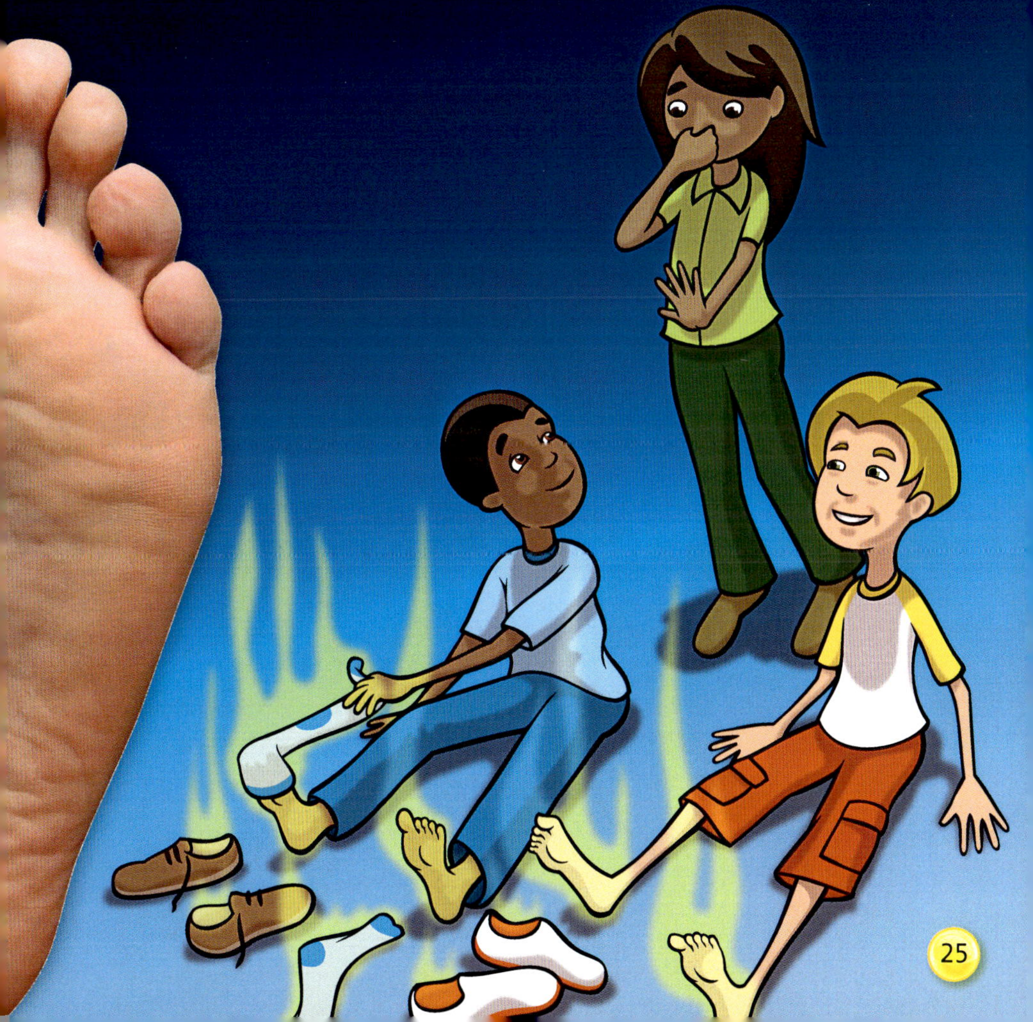

Your Gross Trail

As you read this, your body is dropping gross things. Every day we each lose dead skin. Every year we lose 1.5 million skin flakes!

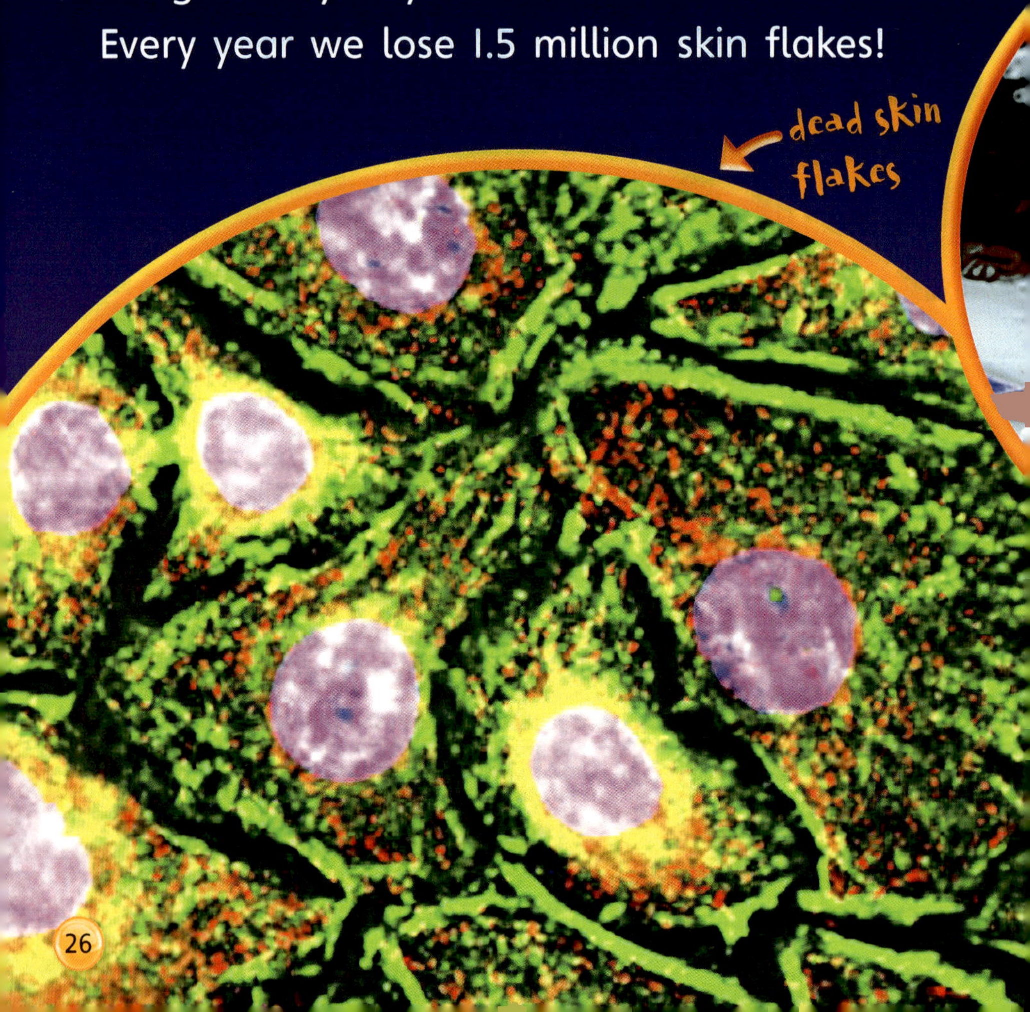

dead skin flakes

Most of what you think is dust is made up of skin flakes. You **shed** them, your pets shed them and your friends shed them. That means we're walking around in a cloud of dead skin flakes. **Gross!**

Gross Stuff

How much **gross stuff** do you remember? Try this **Gross Quiz**.

1 The bacteria in your mouth:

a make an acid that causes your teeth to rot

b eat the food before you do

c make your food taste better

Gross Joke

Q What goes "Ha, ha, plop!"?

A Someone laughing their head off.

2 **On just one foot, there are:**

a only a few sweat glands

b thousands of sweat glands

c no sweat glands, just bacteria

3 **What is snot?**

a bacteria

b dust

c mucus

Gross Joke

Q What poo smells nice?

A Shampoo!

Gross Quiz Answers
1 a 2 b 3 c

All Things Gross

Well done! You made it to the end of the book. We are gross from our heads to our toes! You are now an expert on all things gross. Tell a friend. **Gross them out!**

Glossary

acid	a harsh chemical that tastes sour and can break down other materials
bacteria	the most simple living things, which help material rot and change
dust mites	very small creatures that live in our carpet and bedding, and which eat our dead skin flakes
ear canal	a passage that links the outer ear with the eardrum
gross	revolting, disgusting
intestines	tube-like parts of the body below the stomach
lining	a protective covering on the inside
membranes	soft tissue that lines or connects organs in our bodies
microscope	an instrument that helps you to see very small things by enlarging them
mucus	sticky liquid made in different parts of our bodies
shed	get rid of
skyscraper	very tall office or apartment building with many levels
sweat glands	parts of the body that make and release sweat

bacteria	4–5, 14–15, 22–23, 24–25
ear canal	6
earwax	6–9
feet	24–25
intestines	22
mouth	14–15
mucus	10–13, 16–17
nose	10–13
poo	22–23
skin	4, 26
skin flakes	26–27
stomach	16–17, 18–19, 20–21, 22
sugar	14–15
teeth	15
vomit	20–21